BEHIND THE CURTAIN
Act Out History's BIGGEST Dramas

I0881184

FIGHTING THE MONARCHY

BATTLE OF BUNKER HILL

Virginia Loh-Hagan

45th Parallel Press

Published in the United States of America by Cherry Lake Publishing
Ann Arbor, Michigan
www.cherrylakepublishing.com

Reading Adviser: Marla Conn MS, Ed., Literacy specialist, Read-Ability, Inc.
Book Designer: Felicia Macheske

Photo Credits: © zimmytws/Shutterstock.com, cover, 1; © Dennis W Donohue/Shutterstock.com, cover, 1; Library of Congress, LC-USZC4-4970, 5; Library of Congress, LC-DIG-pga-06114, 6; © Nastasic/iStock.com, 11; Library of Congress, LC-DIG-pga-01711, 12; © KathySG/Shutterstock.com, 17; © flysnowfly/Shutterstock.com, 18; Library of Congress, LC-DIG-ppmsca-19861, 21; Library of Congress, LC-DIG-pga-07229, 23; © Kevin M. McCarthy/Shutterstock.com, 24; © weera sreesam/Shutterstock.com, 29

Graphic Elements Throughout: © Chipmunk131/Shutterstock.com; © Nowik Sylwia/Shutterstock.com; © Andrey_Popov/Shutterstock.com; © NadzeyaShanchuk/Shutterstock.com; © KathyGold/Shutterstock.com; © Black creator/Shutterstock.com; © Edvard Molnar/Shutterstock.com; © Elenadesign/Shutterstock.com; © estherpoon/Shutterstock.com

Copyright © 2019 by Cherry Lake Publishing
All rights reserved. No part of this book may be reproduced or utilized in any form or by any means without written permission from the publisher.

45th Parallel Press is an imprint of Cherry Lake Publishing.

Library of Congress Cataloging-in-Publication Data

Names: Loh-Hagan, Virginia, author.
Title: Fighting the monarchy : Battle of Bunker Hill / Virginia Loh-Hagan.
Description: [Ann Arbor, Michigan] : Cherry Lake Publishing, [2019] | Series: Behind the curtain | Audience: Grade 4 to 6. | Includes bibliographical references and index.
Identifiers: LCCN 2018035564| ISBN 9781534143371 (hardcover) | ISBN 9781534139930 (pbk.) | ISBN 9781534141131 (pdf) | ISBN 9781534142336 (hosted ebook)
Subjects: LCSH: Bunker Hill, Battle of, Boston, Mass., 1775—Juvenile literature. | United States—History—Revolution, 1775-1783—Juvenile literature.
Classification: LCC E241.B9 L64 2019 | DDC 973.3/312–dc23
LC record available at https://lccn.loc.gov/2018035564

Cherry Lake Publishing would like to acknowledge the work of The Partnership for 21st Century Skills. Please visit www.p21.org for more information.

Printed in the United States of America
Corporate Graphics

A Note on Dramatic Retellings

Participating in Readers Theater, or dramatic retellings, can greatly improve reading skills, especially fluency. The books in the **BEHIND THE CURTAIN** series give readers opportunities to learn about important historical events in a fun and engaging way. These books serve as a bridge to more complex texts. All the characters are real figures from history; however, their stories have been fictionalized. To learn more about the people and the events, check out the Viewpoints and Perspectives series and the Perspectives Library series, as the **BEHIND THE CURTAIN** books are aligned to these stories.

TABLE of CONTENTS

HISTORICAL BACKGROUND

At first, Great Britain owned the 13 **colonies**. **Colonists** thought British laws were unfair. They wanted **independence**. They wanted to be their own country. They fought the British. This war was called the American **Revolution**. It was fought from 1775 to 1783. The American colonists won. They became the United States of America.

The Battle of Bunker Hill was one of the first battles of the American Revolution. It took place on June 17, 1775. It was fought in Boston.

Hills surrounded Boston Harbor. British armies wanted to control the hills. This would give them a powerful position to attack. The colonists didn't want this to happen. They built forts on the hills.

FLASH FACT!

After losing battles at Lexington and Concord in April 1775, British forces wanted Bunker Hill to better control Boston.

Vocabulary

colonies (KAH-luh-neez) areas controlled by another country

colonists (KAH-luh-nists) people who live in colonies

independence (in-dih-PEN-duhns) freedom from outside rule

revolution (rev-uh-LOO-shuhn) an overthrow of a government

FLASH FACT!

About 300 British soldiers and officers were killed. About 800 were wounded.

Vocabulary

retreated (rih-TREET-id) quit and backed out

ammunition (am-yuh-NISH-uhn) bullets and gunpowder

combat (KAHM-bat) fight

wounded (WOOND-id) hurt

In the first attack, the colonists fired at the British. The British **retreated**. The British attacked again. The colonists fired. The British retreated. But the colonists ran out of **ammunition**. The British attacked for the third time. The colonists marched out to meet them. They fought in hand-to-hand **combat**. The colonists retreated. The British had more soldiers.

The British won this battle. But they lost more people. Over 1,000 British soldiers were dead or **wounded**. About 450 colonists were dead or wounded. This was the bloodiest battle of the war.

Even though the colonists lost the battle, they felt confident. They realized they could fight against British armies. The Battle of Bunker Hill proved they had the skills to win a war.

CAST of CHARACTERS

NARRATOR: person who helps tell the story

GENERAL THOMAS GAGE: British military commander in charge of all British forces in North America, military governor of Massachusetts

SIMON LAWRENCE: British soldier who is loyal to England

MOLLY WHITAKER: owner of the Green Dragon **Tavern**, American colonist

ABIGAIL ADAMS: American colonist, future U.S. **First Lady**, wife of President John Adams, mother of President John Quincy Adams

SAMUEL CHASE: **minuteman**, American colonist

SALEM POOR: former **slave** who bought his freedom, minuteman who fought with American colonists

BACKSTORY
SPOTLIGHT BIOGRAPHY

Native Americans fought alongside American colonists at the Battle of Bunker Hill. One of them was Samuel Ashbow Jr. He was born around 1746. He was from the Mohegan tribe. The Mohegans lived in the Connecticut area. Ashbow was one of four brothers who fought and died in the American Revolution. Ashbow was 29 years old when he joined the colonists. He was ordered to guard the colonists' fort. During the last attack, Ashbow died. No one knows where he is buried. British soldiers probably buried him in a mass grave. Mass graves are pits. They're dug in the ground. They hold large numbers of dead bodies. Ashbow was the first Native American to die in the American Revolution. He had a wife and son.

Vocabulary

tavern (TAV-urn) restaurant

First Lady (FURST LAY-dee) the wife of a U.S. president

minuteman (MIN-it-man) a person who joined the army of colonists and who could be ready to fight with a minute's notice

slave (SLAYV) someone forced to do work

FLASH FACT!

Abigail Adams was born Abigail Smith in 1744.

ACT 1

NARRATOR: *It's June 1775. It's a few days before the Battle of Bunker Hill. Things are* ***tense*** *between Great Britain and the American colonies.* **GENERAL THOMAS GAGE** *and* **SIMON LAWRENCE** *are at the Green Dragon Tavern. They're sitting at a table talking*

THOMAS: These colonists are causing all kinds of trouble. Who do they think they are?

SIMON: Well, sir, they think the British government is being unfair.

THOMAS: As loyal British **subjects**, we must all obey the laws and pay **taxes**. They can't go around throwing tea off ships. They can't form their own government. They're under our rule!

SIMON: Yes, you're right. We fought in the French and the Seven Years' War. We did this to protect them. It cost a lot of money to fight in wars. They owe us. Also, that tea was really **expensive**. We're only taxing them to get our money back.

Vocabulary

tense (TENS) edgy, on bad terms

subjects (SUHB-jikts) citizens ruled by a king or queen

taxes (TAKS-ez) fees on goods and services

expensive (ik-SPEN-siv) costing a lot of money

FLASH FACT!

Colonists protested against taxes on tea during the Boston Tea Party.

THOMAS: These **rebels** need to be stopped. They need to be punished. They need law and order.

SIMON: I agree. But why not let them have a voice in government? The colonists just want **representation**.

THOMAS: It's our job to lead them. Our king knows what's best for them.

SIMON: But the colonists are really unhappy. What if we work with them?

THOMAS: I tried to talk to their leaders. They just won't listen to **reason**.

SIMON: They're forming secret groups to fight us. I heard some of the rebels are building forts on the hills. Things don't look good.

THOMAS: Forts?! How dare they! We need those hills. We can see the whole city from those hills. The hills give us good **access** to the Boston Harbor.

SIMON: If things don't change, we might be fighting in a war.

Vocabulary

rebels (REB-uhlz) people who fight against those in power

representation (rep-rih-zen-TAY-shuhn) the state of having an elected person acting on the behalf of others

reason (REE-zuhn) logic, common sense

access (AK-ses) a way to enter a place

FLASH FACT!

The Sons of Liberty met to discuss ways to fight British rule.

THOMAS: Do these colonists really think they can fight us? The British army is the most powerful in the world. These rebels are a bunch of farmers and fishermen. They don't even have real uniforms.

SIMON: That may be. But they fought us at Lexington and Concord. I fear Bunker Hill may be next.

THOMAS: This nonsense must be stopped. Send 2,300 soldiers to the hill. Major General William Howe will lead the charge.

NARRATOR: *At that moment,* **MOLLY WHITAKER** *goes to their table. She's the owner of the tavern.*

MOLLY: Gentleman, would you like more to eat or drink?

THOMAS: Molly, it's great that you're here. Do you know about the new **Quartering Act**?

MOLLY: Oh no! Not another one of your British laws!

LOCATION SHOOTING

REAL-WORLD SETTING

The Bunker Hill Monument was built to honor those who died at the Battle of Bunker Hill. It's 221 feet (67 meters) tall. It has 294 steps. It's made of granite. Granite is a smooth stone. The Bunker Hill Monument is an obelisk. Obelisks are stone columns. They look like square pencils. In 1823, a group was formed. It was called the Bunker Hill Monument Association. Building started that year. But the group ran out of money. It had to stop building twice. Land around the monument was sold to raise money. Sarah Josepha Hale also helped raise some money. She was a magazine editor. She wrote "Mary Had a Little Lamb." She organized a fair. The monument was completed in 1842. It was one of the first in the United States.

Vocabulary

Quartering Act (KWOR-tur-ing AKT) a law which required providing of homes and services to soldiers

FLASH FACT!

Minutemen fought to protect their towns. They joined forces to form a militia.

THOMAS: Colonists need to let British soldiers live in their homes. They need to feed them. They need to give them a place to sleep.

MOLLY: This law doesn't make any sense. The British government should house their own soldiers.

THOMAS: It's your **duty**. Think of this as a great honor! And this is your new guest. Meet Simon Lawrence. He'll be quartered at your house.

NARRATOR: **MOLLY WHITAKER** *goes over to the house of* **ABIGAIL ADAMS**.

MOLLY: Can you believe it? Now, we have to serve these British soldiers. We even have to sew their clothes. And we have to do their **laundry**.

ABIGAIL: How do you know this? Who told you?

MOLLY: General Gage and one of his soldiers were at my tavern today. Gage assigned someone to my house.

Vocabulary

duty (DOO-tee) responsibility

laundry (LAWN-dree) the cleaning of clothes

FLASH FACT!

British soldiers took food and supplies from colonists' homes.

ABIGAIL: The days of British soldiers and Boston men sharing food and drink are coming to an end.

MOLLY: Those days are already over. I didn't think I was a rebel. I was born and raised in England. But what the British are doing is unfair. They have taken over our city. There's not enough food. There's not enough to drink. There are too many laws.

ABIGAIL: And now, we have to serve these soldiers who are fighting our men.

MOLLY: I'm a **patriot** now. I don't want to fight in a war. I don't want to lose our men. But I want independence from British rule.

ABIGAIL: Many people feel the same way. I, too, am a patriot. Wait until I tell my husband about this. John and his friends have been talking about forming a new country.

Vocabulary

patriot (PAY-tree-uht) an American colonist who wants independence from British rule

FLASH FACT!

The home where John Adams was born still stands today.

ACT 2

NARRATOR: *It's June 16, 1775, the night before the Battle of Bunker Hill.* **SAMUEL CHASE** *and* **SALEM POOR** *are minutemen. They're at the battle site.*

SAMUEL: What are we doing here? How can I help?

SALEM: Dig these **trenches**. Set up these **railings**. Stuff them with hay. Pack them tightly. Make sure there aren't any gaps.

SAMUEL: It looks like we'll be doing this all night.

SALEM: We need to build a strong fort. If the British want this hill, they're going to have to fight us for it.

SAMUEL: Aren't you worried? There's only 1,200 of us. And there's 2,300 British soldiers. Plus, did you see their warships?

SALEM: We're fighting for our freedom. I was a former slave. I fought hard for my freedom. I'm not going to lose it to the British.

Vocabulary

trenches (TRENCH-iz) long, narrow ditches

railings (RAYL-ingz) fences or walls that serve as barriers

FLASH FACT!

British ships in Boston Harbor fired on colonists as they built forts on the hill.

SAMUEL: I heard men from all the colonies are joining the fight. But I don't see them.

SALEM: It's okay. We have a major **advantage**. We're at the top of the hill. The British have to fight uphill. Plus, these trenches and railings will protect us.

NARRATOR: *It's June 17, 1775. It's the day of the Battle of Bunker Hill.*

SAMUEL: I see them. The soldiers are marching up the hill!

SALEM: Fire at them! Shoot them down!

SAMUEL: I can't see anything. There's so much smoke from the guns and cannons. What's happening?

SALEM: The British are retreating. Oh, wait! They're charging at us again! Shoot them down!

SAMUEL: They're retreating again.

SALEM: We might win!

SAMUEL: What did the **colonel** say?

Vocabulary

advantage (uhd-VAN-tij) benefit

colonel (KUR-nuhl) military officer with a high rank

FLASH FACT!

British soldiers carried 60 pounds (27 kilograms) of equipment uphill.

SALEM: He said to not shoot until we see the **whites** of the British soldiers' eyes.

SAMUEL: What does that mean?

SALEM: We need to save our ammunition. We're running out of bullets and gunpowder.

SAMUEL: It's time to fight with our fists. We can also throw rocks at them.

SALEM: Let's do it! This day will be ours!

NARRATOR: *There are too many British soldiers. The colonists retreat. They escape to the bottom of the hill. They let the British soldiers take the hill.*

SALEM: Why are you so happy? The British won.

SAMUEL: We may have lost that battle. But we're not losers. We put up a good fight. We're just a bunch of **regular** men. The British are **professional** soldiers. And we showed them!

Vocabulary

whites (WITES) white part of the eyeballs

regular (REG-yuh-lur) normal, untrained

professional (pruh-FESH-uh-nuhl) trained

FLASH FACT!

The fighting was wild. Men used bayonets. Bayonets are long guns with swords attached to them.

NARRATOR: *The battle just ended.* **GENERAL THOMAS GAGE** *and* **SIMON LAWRENCE** *are at the top of the hill.*

SIMON: I've never seen such fighting. The rebels don't follow any rules of battles. They just kept firing at us.

THOMAS: That was **brutal**. It was too close. The only reason why the rebels retreated is because they ran out of ammunition.

SIMON: Men fighting for freedom are much stronger than men fighting on a king's orders. But at least we won.

THOMAS: We didn't really win. We lost many more men than they did. The cost of the war is greater than the benefits. It'll take us time to **rebuild** our troops.

SIMON: These colonists don't seem to be too upset about losing.

THOMAS: Yes, they will be encouraged by this.

BLOOPERS

HISTORICAL MISTAKES

The Battle of Bunker Hill wasn't actually fought on Bunker Hill. It was fought on Breed's Hill. Breed's Hill is close to Bunker Hill. It's about one-third of a mile (536 m) south of Bunker Hill. It's closer to Boston. But it's a smaller hill. It's 62 feet (19 m) tall. Colonel William Prescott led the colonists' army. He was told to build a fort on Bunker Hill. He marched to Breed's Hill instead of Bunker Hill. Did Prescott ignore orders? Or did Prescott not know his hills? Or did he get lost in the dark? Or did he get maps that were wrong? People don't know what really happened. Most of the battle was fought on Breed's Hill. But the battle was named for the targeted hill, Bunker Hill.

Vocabulary

brutal (BROO-tuhl) tough

rebuild (ree-BILD) get more men

FLASH FACT!

Bunker Hill is 110 feet (33 m) tall.

NARRATOR: *It's a few days after the Battle of Bunker Hill.* **MOLLY WHITAKER** *and* **ABIGAIL ADAMS** *are at the Green Dragon Tavern.*

ABIGAIL: The battle was so bloody. So many people died.

MOLLY: It's awful. I turned my rooms upstairs into a hospital. Many of our soldiers are still healing.

ABIGAIL: We watched from a hill on our farm. At first, we thought the loud sounds were thunder. My son held my hand and cried.

MOLLY: I'm afraid we're going to lose many of our husbands and sons to this war.

ABIGAIL: This war affects us all. We women will have to take over our husbands' work.

MOLLY: One day, we'll be a free country.

ABIGAIL: The lives lost at the Battle of Bunker Hill have paid **dearly** for that freedom.

Vocabulary
dearly (DEER-lee) very much, greatly

FLASH FACT!
The colonists used trench warfare. This was rare prior to the American Revolution.

EVENT TIMELINE

- **March 24, 1765:** The Quartering Act is passed. Colonists don't like this law.
- **August 1765:** The Sons of Liberty is formed. This is a secret group of patriots. The Sons of Liberty fight against unfair English laws. In Boston, Samuel Adams leads the Sons of Liberty.
- **March 5, 1770:** The Boston Massacre takes place. Massacre is the killing of many people at the same time. A crowd of colonists bully a British soldier. Other soldiers come to help him. Shots break out. Five colonists are killed.
- **December 16, 1773:** The Boston Tea Party takes place. The Sons of Liberty destroy a shipment of tea. They throw tea into the sea. They opposed tea taxes.
- **March 1774:** The British government passes the Coercive Acts. Coercive means being forceful. These laws punish colonists for not obeying British rule. The colonists call these laws the Intolerable Acts. Intolerable means too bad to handle.
- **April 19, 1775:** The Battles of Lexington and Concord take place. These are the first military battles of the American Revolution. Paul Revere warns the patriots that the British are coming.
- **May 10, 1775:** American colonists attack Fort Ticonderoga, which is controlled by British soldiers. They capture the fort. This is the first American victory. The Americans take the weapons.
- **June 14, 1775:** The Continental army is created. George Washington commands the army. Soldiers from all 13 colonies join.
- **June 17, 1775:** The British attack Breed's Hill and Bunker Hill. The Battle of Bunker Hill takes place.
- **August 23, 1775:** King George III of Great Britain hears about the Battle of Bunker Hill. He declares that the colonies are in a state of "open and avowed rebellion." Avowed means stated publicly.

CONSIDER THIS!

TAKE A POSITION! A Pyrrhic victory means winning at a great cost. Some people think the Battle of Bunker Hill was a Pyrrhic victory for the British. Why do you think that is? Do you agree or disagree? Argue your point with reasons and evidence.

SAY WHAT? Learn more about the role of African Americans at the Battle of Bunker Hill. Explain their roles. Explain their significance.

THINK ABOUT IT! Ever since 1786, Boston has hosted the Bunker Hill Day parade. This takes place on the Sunday on or before June 17. What do you think happens on this day? How would you plan this parade?

LEARN MORE

Burgan, Michael. *The Battle of Bunker Hill: An Interactive History Adventure.* North Mankato, MN: Capstone Press, 2016.

Krull, Kathleen. *A Kid's Guide to the American Revolution.* New York: HarperCollins, 2018.

Lusted, Marcia Amidon. *The Battle of Bunker Hill.* Ann Arbor, MI: Cherry Lake Publishing, 2014.

Russo, Kristin J. *Viewpoints on the Battle of Bunker Hill.* Ann Arbor, MI: Cherry Lake Publishing, 2019.

INDEX

ABOUT THE AUTHOR

Dr. Virginia Loh-Hagan is an author, university professor, and former classroom teacher. She's visited Boston a couple of times. She walked the Freedom Trail. She lives in San Diego with her very tall husband and very naughty dogs. To learn more about her, visit www.virginialoh.com.